✛ ✖ MATHS ➗ ⊖
PROBLEM SOLVING

TRANSPORT

by Anita Loughr

CONTENTS

INTRODUCTION

Context-based maths gives you a purpose for using maths, and cements your understanding of both why and how maths is applied to daily life. This book explores a range of numeracy skills and topics through 13 different real-life scenarios.

At the head of each section, there's a quick visual guide to the topic and skills covered. The introduction to each section sets the scene and presents the maths question that will be answered.

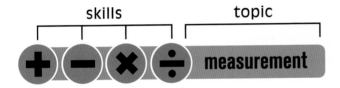

Then you are guided through the process of answering the question, step by step.

In addition, each section also contains helpful tips and an extra challenge: **Now try this ...**

There's an answer key for the **Now try this ...** challenge at the end of the book and words covered in the glossary are highlighted in **bold** throughout the text.

WHAT'S THE CHEAPEST WAY TO TRAVEL?

Your parents have promised you the holiday of a lifetime at an awesome adventure park, but how are you going to get there? You want to make sure it's not too expensive because you'd like to have plenty of spending money. Which of the following types of transport do you think will be best to use and why?

Let's put the different types of transport in price order, from the least to the most expensive.

Least			Most
£40	£58	£80	£108

It looks like travelling by car is going to be the most expensive way to travel. But wait a minute!
The cost of travelling by car is for the whole family.
All of the other travel prices are for one person.

So, you're going to have to multiply each price by 4 to compare them with the cost of going by car.

Bus   £40 × 4 people = £160

Train £58 × 4 people = £232

Plane £80 × 4 people = £320

Now let's put the prices in order again, from the cheapest to the most expensive.

Least			Most
£108	£160	£232	£320

 It definitely looks like going by car is the cheapest way to travel!

Make it easy!

Remove zeros to make sums easier:
$40 \times 4 = ?$
$4 \times 4 = 16$
Then put them back:
$40 \times 4 = 160$

Partition numbers to make things easier:
$58 \times 4 = ?$
$58 = 50 + 8$
$50 \times 4 = 200$
$8 \times 4 = 32$
$58 \times 4 = 232$

Now try this ...

There are 2 friends who want to come with you to the adventure park. You don't have space in your car for 6 people and taking 2 cars is not an option. What is the cheapest way for all of you to get there?

HOW LONG WILL THE JOURNEY TAKE?

You're taking the bus into town with your brother and sister after lunch. The next bus is due at 14.30. You want to work out how long the journey will take so you know how much time you'll have in town.

> There are 24 hours in each day. Some clocks show all 24 hours. They are called **24 hour clocks**. When these clocks go past 12, they carry on counting up to 24. On the 24 hour clock, 12.00 is midday and 00.00 is midnight.

This is what you might see when you wake up and look at your alarm clock.

To work out what this time is on a **12 hour clock**, you need to take away 12. Taking away 10 and then taking away 2 might be easier.

14.30 – 10 = **4.30 and 4.30 – 2 = 2.30**

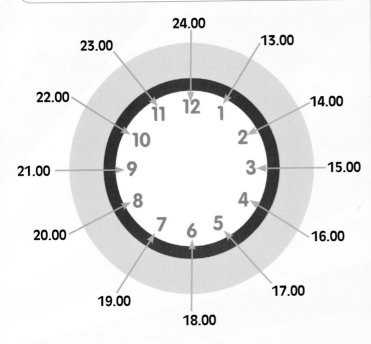

Make it easy!

Take away 12
(or 10 and then 2!)

13.00 – 10 = 3 and
3 – 2 = 1pm
14.00 – 10 = 4 and
4 – 2 = 2pm
15.00 – 10 = 5 and
5 – 2 = 3pm
16.00 – 10 = 6 and
6 – 2 = 4pm
17.00 – 10 = 7 and
7 – 2 = 5pm

The bus timetable says your bus will arrive in town at 15.26. Let's work out how long your journey will take.

Partition blocks of time to make things easier. Don't forget an hour is made up of 60 minutes.

```
      30 minutes        20 minutes      6 minutes
14.30              15.00          15.20      15.26
```

30 + 20 + 6 = 56

Your journey is going to take
56 minutes.

Now try this ...

Oh no! You missed the bus. You have to wait 45 minutes for the next bus. What time will you arrive in town now?

WHICH IS THE SHORTEST ROUTE?

You are going to the park for a fun day out. There are two different routes you can take to get there. Which route do you think will be the best one to take?

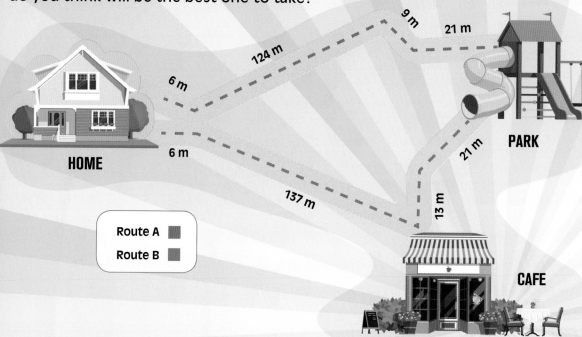

9 m
21 m
124 m
6 m
6 m
137 m
21 m
13 m

HOME
PARK
CAFE

Route A
Route B

You can work out the distance for each route using the **column method**.
First place the distances from Route A into the columns:

Route A

H	T	U
		6
1	2	4 +
		9
	2	1
		0
	2	

H	T	U
		6
1	2	4 +
		9
	2	1
1	6	0
	2	

Add the numbers in the units column (U).

6 + 4 + 9 + 1 = 20

Write 0 in the answer box for the units column and carry the 2 over to the tens column (T).

Now add the tens column: 2 + 2 + 2 carried over = 6

There's nothing to add in the hundreds column! Just write 1 in the answer box.

Route A = 160 m

Do the same for Route B.

Route B

H	T	U			H	T	U	
		6					6	
1	3	7	+		1	3	7	+
	1	3				1	3	
	2	1				2	1	
		7			1	7	7	
	1					1		

Start with the units column: 6 + 7 + 3 + 1 = 17

Write the 7 in the answer box for the units column and carry the 1 over to the tens column.

Now add the tens column:
3 + 1 + 2 + 1 carried over = 7

There's nothing to add in the hundreds column. Just write 1 in the answer box.

Route B = 177 m

If you take the smallest number away from the largest you can see Route A is 17 metres shorter than Route B.

H	T	U	
1	7	7	–
1	6	0	
	1	7	

Route A is the shortest route to the park.

Make it easy!

Write your numbers carefully in the correct **columns** so you don't make any mistakes when you **add up**.

Don't forget to **add** the number you have **carried over** into the **tens column**.

Now try this ...

On the journey you get hungry, so you stop at the café for something to eat. After you have eaten how far do you still have to travel to get to the park?

WHAT DIRECTION ARE YOU GOING?

After school, you are meeting your friend at the swimming pool. You know how to get there, but what direction are you travelling?

The most important direction on a compass is north (N) as the needle always points in this direction. The other **compass points** are east (E), south (S) and west (W).

You can use a **mnemonic** to help remember which order the directions are in, such as:

Never Eat Slimy Worms

or

Naughty Elephants Squirt Water

A compass measures in degrees (°).

A full turn from north back to north is 360°.

East is 90° clockwise away from north.

South is 180° clockwise away from north.

West is 90° anti-clockwise away from north.

But if you turn 45° clockwise or anti-clockwise away from north and south which directions will you be facing?

Halfway between north and east is the direction called north-east (NE).

Halfway between north and west is the direction called north-west (NW).

Halfway between south and east is the direction called south-east (SE).

Halfway between south and west is the direction called south-west (SW).

To get to the swimming pool after school you need to go south, east, south and east, taking three **right angle** turns.

 You are travelling south-east from the school to the swimming pool.

Make it easy!

Clockwise is the same direction as the hands of a clock move. Anti-clockwise is the opposite direction.

anti-clockwise   clockwise

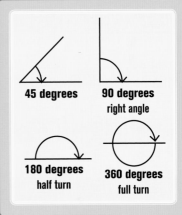

45 degrees

90 degrees
right angle

180 degrees
half turn

360 degrees
full turn

Now try this ...

After your swim you are going to watch a movie. Which direction do you travel in from the swimming pool to the cinema?

HOW MUCH FUEL DOES MUM NEED?

Your mum is going on a motorbike trip and you want to help her work out how much fuel she's going to need. Her motorbike uses 3 litres of fuel to travel 45 kilometres. How many litres will it need to go 450 kilometres?

If you divide the distance by the amount of fuel you will find out how far the motorbike can travel on 1 litre of fuel.

$45 \div 3 = 15$

So 1 litre of fuel is enough to travel 15 kilometres.

To work out how much fuel the motorbike would need to travel 450 kilometres you divide the total distance it needs to travel by the distance it can travel on one litre of fuel.

$450 \div 15 = 30$

So to travel 450 kilometres your mum will need 30 litres of fuel.

The fuel tank only holds 24 litres of fuel.
Your mum will need to stop for more fuel.

How much more fuel will be needed for the motorbike to reach its destination?

To work this out, take away how much the tank holds from the total amount of fuel needed to get there.

$30 - 24 = 6$

Make it easy!

Use inverse operations to check your answers:
$450 \div 15 = 30$
$30 \times 15 = 450$

Choose the **correct operation** (multiplication, division, addition, subtraction) to work out the **sum**.

Look for clues in the questions:

For 'How much more fuel… ?' you need to use **addition** or **subtraction**.

Now try this ...

How much fuel would be needed for the journey if the motorbike used 5 **litres** of fuel to go 45 **kilometres**? Is this better or worse?

So your mum will need 30 litres of fuel and she'll have to stop to get an extra 6 litres along the way.

WHEN IS THE QUIETEST TIME TO DRIVE THROUGH TOWN?

Your judo club runs classes every Saturday morning, afternoon and evening. It's across town so you want to work out the best time for your dad to give you a lift. The charts below show the amount of transport on the road at different times of the day. Use them to help you!

MORNING

Motorbike	JHT I
Car	JHT JHT JHT II
Bus	JHT
Van	JHT III
Lorry	II

AFTERNOON

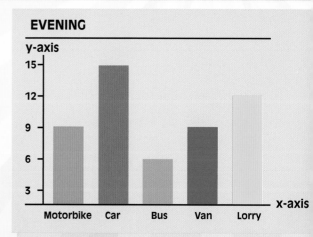

Motorbike	
Car	
Bus	
Van	
Lorry	

EVENING

y-axis

15 –
12 –
9 –
6 –
3 –

Motorbike   Car   Bus   Van   Lorry

x-axis

The MORNING chart is a **tally** chart. Tally marks record numbers in groups of 5 which makes it easy to count the numbers and find out the total.

First, count all the groups of 5 in the chart. There are 6 of them. 6 × 5 = 30

Next, count all the single tally marks. There are 8.

Add both numbers to find out the total number of vehicles travelling in the morning. 30 + 8 = 38

38 vehicles were travelling on the road in the morning.

Make it easy!

The fifth **tally mark** in a group crosses the other four so it's easier to **count up** the **total** amount.

The AFTERNOON chart is a **pictogram**. Pictograms show data in pictures. You count the pictures in each row to find the quantity of each vehicle.

Motorbike	Car	Bus	Van	Lorry
1	11	4	2	7

First, add the smallest units together. 1 + 1 + 4 + 2 = 8

Add this to the remaining unit, 7.
8 + 7 = 15

Now add this total to the 10 – there's only one.

15 + 10 = 25

25 vehicles were travelling on the road in the afternoon.

Always look for a key in **pictograms** because a single picture can often represent a big number. Always look at the **scale** on the **y-axis** in **bar charts** because the gaps can represent big numbers too.

The EVENING chart is a **bar chart**. Bar charts show data in columns. You read the number at the top of each column to see the quantity of each vehicle.

Motorbike	Car	Bus	Van	Lorry
9	15	6	9	12

First, add the smallest units together: 5 + 6 + 2 = 13

Next add the larger units together. 9 + 9 = 18

Then, add up the tens. 10 + 10 = 20

Finally, add all of your totals together. 20 + 18 + 13 = 51

51 vehicles were travelling on the road in the evening.

Now try this ...

How many vehicles were there in total that day?

The afternoon is the best time to travel because that's when the roads are quietest.

HOW MANY CARS ARE THERE?

You're organising a sponsored car wash with your friends.
The car park has 4 floors. 128 cars can park on each floor.
How many cars can go in the car park altogether?

You can work out how many cars can fit into the car park by **multiplying** the number of car parking spaces by the number of floors. Use the **column method** to organise your numbers.

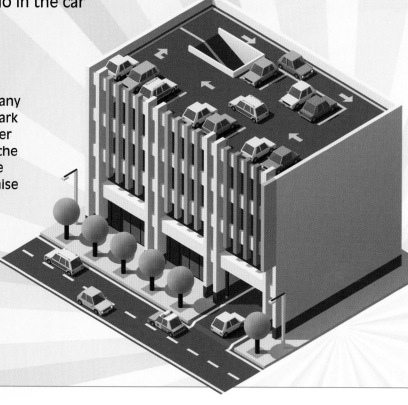

H	T	U	
1	2	8	
		4	×
		2	
	3		

$8 \times 4 = 32$ — Write 2 in the units column answer box and carry the 3 tens over into the tens column.

H	T	U	
1	2	8	
		4	×
5	1	2	
1	3		

$2 \times 4 = 8$ — Remember to add the 3 carried over.

$8 + 3 = 11$ — Write 1 in the tens column answer box and carry over the one hundred.

$1 \times 4 = 4$ — Then add the one hundred carried over.

$4 + 1 = 5$ — Write 5 in the answer box in the hundreds column.

There is room for 512 cars in the car park. The car park attendant tells you there are 13 empty spaces on each floor.

How many cars are there in the car park?

```
H  T  U
   1  3
      4  ×
   ─────
      2
   1
```
$3 \times 4 = 12$

Write 2 in the units column answer box and carry the 1 ten over into the tens column.

```
H  T  U
   1  3
      4  ×
   ─────
   5  2
   1
```
$1 \times 4 = 4$

Add the 1 ten you carried over. $4 + 1 = 5$

Write the 5 in the tens column answer box.

There are 52 spaces left. Take 52 away from the total amount of car park spaces to find how many cars are already parked.

```
H  T  U
5  1  2
   5  2  –
   ─────
      0
```
$2 - 2 = 0$

Write 0 in the units column answer box.

```
H  T  U
4 5 ₁1  2
    5  2  –
   ─────
    6  0
```
You can't subtract 50 from 10 so you need to borrow 1 from the hundreds column. Place this 1 in the tens column next to the 1 that's already there. And don't forget to reduce the number in the hundreds column by 1. Now do the sum.

$11 - 5 = 6$

```
H  T  U
4 5 ₁1  2
    5  2  –
   ─────
 4  6  0
```
Write 6 in the answer box at the bottom of the tens column.

There's 4 left in the hundreds column. There's nothing to take away from it so you can just write it in the answer box.

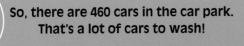

So, there are 460 cars in the car park. That's a lot of cars to wash!

Make it easy!

Always start with the **units column** when you're using the **column method**.

Don't forget to **add** the number **carried over** when you're using the **column method**.

Now try this ...

35 of the empty spaces in the car park are reserved.

How many empty spaces are left?

HOW FAR DOES SHE DRIVE ... APPROXIMATELY?

Your aunt is a lorry driver. She travels from Oxford to Liverpool and home again every day, 5 days a week. It is 268 kilometres each way. She says she drives thousands of kilometres each week but you want more detail. How many kilometres does your aunt travel each week, to the nearest 1,000?

Oxford   268 km

If your aunt travels home and back every day, she does the journey twice a day for 5 days a week. This means she travels 268 kilometres 10 times a week. To work out how many kilometres she travels each week you have to multiply 268 by 10.

268 × 10 = 2,680

To round this to the nearest 100 you have to check the number in the tens column. If it is 5 or more the number in the hundreds column is rounded up. If it is less than 5 it is rounded down.

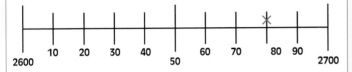

So 2,680 to the nearest 100 is 2,700 hundred. Your aunt drives approximately 2,700 kilometres each week.

But how far does she travel to the nearest 1,000? To round to the nearest 1,000, you have to check the number in the hundreds column. If it is 5 or more the number in the thousands column is rounded up. If it is less than 5 it is rounded down.

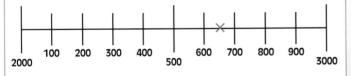

So 2,680 to the nearest 1,000 is 3,000.

Now you know your aunt drives approximately 3,000 kilometres each week.

Make it easy!

When **multiplying** by 10 we can simply **add** a zero to the original number.

268 × 10 = 268**0**
456 × 10 = 456**0**

If the number ends in 5 or above **round** it **up**. If it ends in 4 or below **round** it **down**.

Now try this ...

What happens if you **round up** the number of kilometres before you **calculate** the **total** distance travelled?

19

HOW MUCH IS THAT FRACTION EXACTLY?

On a trip into London, you've counted 64 passengers in your carriage. At a glance, half are chatting, a quarter are listening to music and an eighth are reading. The other eighth are looking out of the window. But exactly how many people are doing each of these things?

To work out a **fraction** of a whole number, divide it by the bottom number in the fraction. The bottom number in a fraction is called the **denominator**.

½ of 64 = 64 ÷ 2 = 32
So 32 of the passengers are chatting.

To find out how many passengers are listening to music you need to divide 64 by the denominator in ¼. The denominator of ¼ is 4.

64 ÷ 4 = 16

So 16 people are listening to music on the train.

How many passengers are reading? Divide 64 by the denominator of ⅛.

64 ÷ 8 = 8

8 people are reading.

The same fraction of passengers are looking out of the window so you know that exactly 8 people are also looking out of the window.

Make it easy!

To **calculate fractions** of things **divide** them by the **denominator**.
For ½ **divide** by 2.
For ¼ **divide** by 4.
For ⅛ **divide** by 8.

You can represent **data** in a **pie chart** so it's easy to understand.

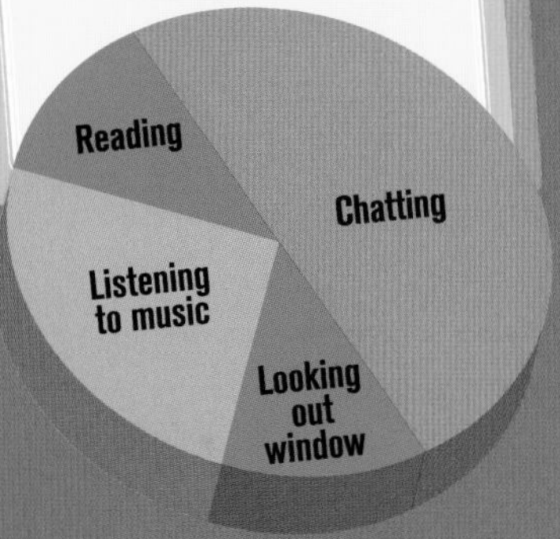

Reading

Chatting

Listening to music

Looking out window

1							
½				½			
¼		¼		¼		¼	
⅛	⅛	⅛	⅛	⅛	⅛	⅛	⅛

32 people are chatting, 16 are listening to music, 8 are reading and another 8 are staring out of the window.

Now try this ...

If a **quarter** of the passengers chatting get off at the next station, how many passengers are still on the train?

21

WHAT DISTANCE DO YOU TRAVEL AROUND THE ISLAND?

You have just been on a short boat ride around an island. You want to work out the distance you have travelled. The boat ride takes an hour and the captain can tell you the speed the boat was going. You'll have to work out the rest yourself!

Your boat travelled 32 kilometres an hour for the first 15 minutes, 46 kilometres an hour for the next 30 minutes and 28 kilometres an hour for the last 15 minutes.

You know the whole trip took an hour. To find out the total distance travelled you will need to work out the distance for each stage of the journey.

The FIRST stage of the journey was 15 minutes which is the same as a quarter of an hour.
60 minutes ÷ 15 minutes = 4

To work out the distance travelled for this first stage, divide 32 kilometres by 4.

32 ÷ 4 = 8

The SECOND stage of the journey took half an hour.

60 minutes ÷ 30 minutes = 2
So divide the distance travelled by 2.

46 ÷ 2 = 23

For the LAST stage of the journey you have to work out how much time had already been travelled and subtract it from the total time it took.

15 minutes + 30 minutes = 45 minutes

60 minutes – 45 minutes = 15 minutes

You already know you need to divide the speed by 4 to work out how far the boat travelled in 15 minutes.

28 ÷ 4 = 7

To find the total distance travelled, add up all your totals.

8 + 23 + 7 = 38

The distance you travelled around the island is 38 kilometres.

Make it easy!

Convert hours into minutes:

1 hour = 60 minutes
½ an hour = 30 minutes
¼ of an hour = 15 minutes

To **convert metres** into **kilometres, divide** by 1,000.
To **convert kilometres** to metres, **multiply** by 1,000.

Now try this ...

Another boat travels at a constant **speed** of 40 **kilometres** an hour for 60 **minutes**. How far does it travel in **metres**?

WHEN ARE WE GOING TO ARRIVE?

You're travelling by ferry from Roscoff to Plymouth at the end of a school trip. The captain has just announced you'll be arriving 13 minutes earlier than expected. You want to text your mum with the new arrival time but first you need to work it out!

06.00

The ferry left Roscoff at 22.30. The journey usually takes 8 hours but it's going to arrive 13 minutes early because of good sailing conditions. What time will it arrive in Plymouth?

First you need to work out the scheduled arrival time and then you need to subtract 13 minutes from it.

The journey took 8 hours and crossed midnight into morning. At midnight the 24 hour clock shows 00.00.

Count 8 hours on from 22.30, remembering that after 00.00, the 24 hour clock starts back at 1 again. You can also use the analogue clock below to help you.

22.30, 23.30, 00.30, 01.30, 02.30, 03.00, 04.30, 05.30, 06.30

You are scheduled to arrive at 06.30 but your ferry is going to arrive 13 minutes earlier than that.

So you need to subtract 13 minutes from 30 minutes to find out when you actually arrived. Partitioning will help you work this out. 13 = 10 + 3

30 – 10 = 20 and 20 – 3 = 17

So your ferry is going to dock in Plymouth at 06.17.

Make it easy!

There are 24 hours in a day and 60 minutes in an hour.

Partition hours and minutes to help you calculate sums.

Now try this ...

If the ferry arrived 22 minutes late what time would it dock in Plymouth?

HOW MUCH CHANGE WILL I GET?

You are going to visit some friends in Paris and from there you're going to New York on a sight-seeing adventure. It's going to be really exciting but how much change will you get from £1,000 after you've paid for all those flights?

Tags shown on the image:
- NEW YORK TO LONDON £354
- LONDON TO PARIS £86
- PARIS TO NEW YORK £371

Make it easy!

Partitioning numbers makes **calculating easier**

275 = 200 + 70 + 5

Subtract the smaller number from the larger number to find the difference.

You need to add up the prices to find the total cost. You can do this by partitioning.

First add up the hundreds. 300 + 300 = 600
Next add up the tens. 70 + 50 + 80 = 200
Then add up the units. 1 + 4 + 6 = 11
Last add up the totals. 600 + 200 + 11 = 811

You now need to take away the total cost of the journey from £1,000 to find out how much change you will have left.

Use partitioning to help you. Partition 811 into 800, 10 and 1.
1000 − 800 = 200 and 200 − 10 = 190 and 190 − 1 = 189

Now try this ...

A return to New York from London costs £515. How much money will you save if you only visit New York?

So you will get £189 in change.

WHERE ARE WE GOING?

You are going on a mystery tour. All you have been given are the **coordinates** and a grid! Can you work out where you'll be visiting?

Your first stop is (2,6). Where are you going first?

Look at the grid. The **vertical** and **horizontal** lines have been numbered. This is to help you find the places on the grid. In this grid, the numbers on the horizontal line tell us how far across a place is. The numbers on the vertical lines tell us how far up a place is.

You go 2 across on the x-axis and 6 up on the y-axis. The place marked on this spot is the Water Park.

Your next stop is (6,7). Where are you going next? Go 6 across on the x-axis and 7 up on the y-axis. The place marked on this spot is Crazy Golf.

Next you go to (4,2). Where are you going last? Go 4 across and 2 up. For your last stop, you are at the Zoological Gardens.

Make it easy!

In the alphabet, **X** comes before **Y**. When you read **coordinates**, read the number on the **x-axis** and then the number on the **y-axis**.

Another way to remember how to read **coordinates** is the phrase: You walk along the corridor and then up the stairs.

Now try this ...

What are the **coordinates** of Skydive Peaks?

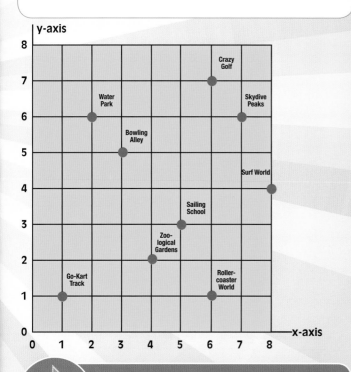

You are going to the Water Park, Crazy Golf and the Zoological Gardens.

GLOSSARY

Axis Lines framing a graph or chart. The horizontal line is called the x-axis. The vertical line is called the y-axis.

Bar chart A chart that displays data using rectangular bars of different heights.

Column method Sums written in vertical lines of hundreds, tens and units so numbers can be carried over and borrowed easily.

Compass points A method of explaining direction using the points of a compass e.g. north, south, east and west.

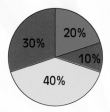

Convert To change a unit of measurement e.g. kilometres (km) to metres (m); centimetres (cm) to millimetres (mm); hours to minutes.

Coordinates Pairs of numbers that show the exact position on a grid, map or graph. The first number shows where a point is on the x-axis. The second number shows where a point is on the y-axis.

Denominator The bottom number of a fraction, e.g. the denominator of ¼ is 4.

Distance The length between two points, measured in kilometres (km), metres (m), centimetres (cm) and millimetres (mm).

Fraction A part of the whole.

Horizontal A line that goes straight across from left to right.

Mnemonic A word, phrase or poem that helps you remember something.

Operation The four mathematical operations are addition (+), subtraction (–), multiplication (x) and division (÷).

Partition To separate numbers into thousands, hundreds, tens and units to make calculations easier.

Pictogram A chart that uses pictures to represent data.

Pie chart A circular chart divided into sections to represent different amounts.

Right angle An angle that is exactly 90°.

Tally Four vertical lines crossed diagonally by a fifth line to represent a group of five. Tally charts are used to collect data quickly.

Motorbike	卌 I
Car	卌 卌 卌 II
Bus	卌
Van	卌 III
Lorry	II

Twelve hour clock A clock showing 1am to 12pm (noon) then 1pm to 12am (midnight).

Twenty four hour clock A clock that shows the time in numbers from 00.00 (midnight) to 23.59.

Vertical A line that goes straight up and down.

NOW TRY THIS ... ANSWERS

Page 5

Bus £40 x 6 = £240
Train £58 x 6 = £364
Plane £80 x 6 = £480
The bus is the cheapest option.

Page 7

The bus you missed arrives in town at 15.26.
15.26 + 45 minutes = 16.11
The next bus arrives at 16.11.

Page 9

It's 13 m + 21 m from the café to the park.
13 + 21 = 34
It's 34 m from the café to the park.

Page 11

From the swimming pool to the cinema, the direction is north-west (NW).

Page 13

If 5 litres are needed to go 45 km,
50 litres would be needed to
go 450 km. 50 litres is more
than 36 litres. It's worse.

Page 15

38 + 25 + 51 = 114 vehicles

There were 114 vehicles in total that day.

Page 17

52 − 35 = 17
There are 17 empty spaces left.

Page 19

270 km x 10 = 2,700
300 km x 10 = 3,000
You get the same answers.

Page 21

Quarter of the people chatting is 8.
32 ÷ 4 = 8
So, 8 people are getting off the train.
There are 56 people left on the train.
64 − 8 = 56

Page 23

1 kilometre = 1,000 metres
40 kilometres = 40,000 metres

Page 25

6.30 am + 22 minutes = 6.52 am
The ferry would arrive at 6.52 am.

Page 27

All your flights cost £811. A flight to New York costs £515.
811 − 515 = 296
You would save £296.

Page 29

The coordinates of Skydive Peaks are (7,6).

Published in paperback in Great Britain in 2020 by Wayland
Copyright © Hodder and Stoughton, 2018
All rights reserved

Produced for Wayland by Dynamo
Written by: Anita Loughrey

ISBN: 978 1 5263 0734 7

Wayland, an imprint of
Hachette Children's Group
Part of Hodder and Stoughton
Carmelite House
50 Victoria Embankment
London EC4Y 0DZ

An Hachette UK Company
www.hachette.co.uk
www.hachettechildrens.co.uk

Printed in China

10 9 8 7 6 5 4 3 2 1

Picture acknowledgements (cover and inside pages): All images and
graphic elements used are courtesy of Shutterstock. Every attempt
has been made to clear copyright. Should there be any inadvertent
omission, please apply to the Publisher for rectification.